ENVIRONMENTAL JOURNALISM

MW01174232

INVESTIGATIVE JOURNALISM THAT INSPIRED CHANGE

DIANE DAKERS

Crabtree Publishing Company

www.crabtreebooks.com

Author: Diane Dakers

Series research and development:
Janine Deschenes and Reagan Miller

Editorial director: Kathy Middleton

Editor: Janine Deschenes

Proofreaders: Wendy Scavuzzo, Melissa Boyce

Design and photo research:
Katherine Berti

Print and production coordinator:
Katherine Berti

Images:

Getty Images: Jim Xu: p. 16
Google Maps: Screen Shot 2018-06-26 at 3.07.55 PM: p. 28
highline.huffingtonpost.com
    Screen Shot 2018-06-27 at 11.37.05 AM: p. 38
NASA, courtesy Goddard Space Flight Center
    Ozone Processing Team: p. 17 (bottom)
peterwklein.com: Screen Shot 2018-06-25 at 4.52.56 PM: p. 20
Shutterstock
    Bjoern Wylezich: p. 1 (top right)
    EQRoy: p. 5 (bottom)
    Erik Cox Photography: p. 35
    Kwasi Kyei Mensah: p. 18 (bottom)
    Lawrey: front cover (newspapers)
    Niloo: p. 11 (top)
    pixinoo: p. 11 (center bottom)
    ricochet64: p. 32
    SAPhotog: p. 6
theintercept.com
    Screen Shot 2018-06-27 at 11.49.47 AM: p. 40
    Screen Shot 2018-06-27 at 12.26.08 PM: p. 41 (center)
UBC Journalism: front cover (top left), p. 15, 18 (top), 19, 21
www.nytimes.com
    Screen Shot 2018-06-27 at 12.32.23 PM: p. 41 (bottom right)
www.revealnews.org
    Screen Shot 2018-06-26 at 1.08.23 PM: p. 26
www.thedevilweknow.com
    Screen Shot 2018-06-27 at 12.27.40 PM: p. 41 (bottom left)
www.worldpressphoto.org
    Screen Shot 2018-06-27 at 12.19.38 PM: p. 41 (top)
All other images by Shutterstock

Library and Archives Canada Cataloguing in Publication

Dakers, Diane, author
        Environmental journalism / Diane Dakers.

(Investigative journalism that inspired change)
Includes bibliographical references and index.
Issued in print and electronic formats.
ISBN 978-0-7787-5349-0 (hardcover).--
ISBN 978-0-7787-5362-9 (softcover).--ISBN 978-1-4271-2196-7 (HTML)

        1. Environmental protection--Press coverage--Juvenile literature.
2. Environmental protection--Press coverage--Case studies--Juvenile
literature. 3. Mass media and the environment--Juvenile literature. I.
Title.

P96.E57D34 2018   j070.4'493637   C2018-905442-5
                                                          C2018-905443-3

Library of Congress Cataloging-in-Publication Data

Available at the Library of Congress

Crabtree Publishing Company
www.crabtreebooks.com   1-800-387-7650

Printed in the U.S.A./122018/CG20181005

**Published
in Canada
Crabtree Publishing**
616 Welland Ave.
St. Catharines, Ontario
L2M 5V6

**Published in the
United States
Crabtree Publishing**
PMB 59051
350 Fifth Avenue, 59th Floor
New York, New York 10118

**Published in the
United Kingdom
Crabtree Publishing**
Maritime House
Basin Road North, Hove
BN41 1WR

**Published
in Australia
Crabtree Publishing**
3 Charles Street
Coburg North
VIC 3058

CONTENTS

INVESTIGATING THE ENVIRONMENT

E-waste is often broken apart to remove **circuit boards** (above). Then, the circuit boards are burned to extract tiny pieces of **precious metal**. The journalists found that children often do these dangerous jobs.

We've all heard the phrase "reduce, reuse, recycle." Most of us do our best to follow this advice, because usually, it benefits the environment and helps save Earth from harmful **waste pollution**. Sometimes, however, our well-meaning activities have results we never could have imagined.

Consumers around the world, for example, recycle or donate millions of tons of old computers, TVs, and other electronic devices every year. Many believe their unwanted electronics will be disposed of in an environmentally safe way, or that parts will be reused. Unfortunately, as a group of Canadian journalism students discovered, much of this so-called "e-waste" is not recycled safely. Some of it is literally killing people on the other side of the world.

The students uncovered this story during an International Reporting class at the University of British Columbia (UBC) on Canada's west coast. For five months, they tracked the trail of unwanted electronics from North America to **developing nations**. There, they found local children sorting, smashing, and burning the cast-off electronics. The kids were cut, scorched, and poisoned in the process.

The students' research for this story took them to three countries on two continents. Their inquiries involved hidden cameras, paper trails, and anonymous **sources**. They also uncovered an unexpected, criminal, offshoot to the e-waste **industry**.

> [The e-waste dump] is essentially this charred, **toxic** wasteland. The ground is just scorched absolutely everywhere. Everywhere you walk, there's **shards** of plastic and metal and glass protruding from the ground.

**Blake Sifton,
student involved in
e-waste documentary**

An investigative journalist does in-depth research and reporting on a specfic topic.

Along with their professor, the students produced a short documentary based on their e-waste investigation. The 24-minute film, *Ghana: Digital Dumping Ground,* earned an Emmy Award in 2010. It also led to public outrage and changes to the rules relating to how e-waste is disposed and recycled around the world.

The story of how the students carried out their investigation is a tale of international intrigue, undercover reporting, and world-changing journalism. It might sound like the plot of a television drama or Hollywood movie. In reality, it's all part of the job for a particular type of news reporter— the investigative journalist.

THE JOURNALIST AND THE J-SCHOOL

A journalist, or reporter, is a person trained to find and present news stories for newspaper, radio, TV, and online audiences. They can recognize news stories when they see them, separate facts from fiction and opinion, ask useful questions, and find sources of information that present all sides of a story.

To learn these skills, most journalists today attend journalism school, often called J-School. Some universities, such as UBC, offer degrees in journalism. Many colleges offer **diploma** programs, and some high schools present journalism classes and workshops. Typically, a journalism program involves classroom studies and hands-on, real-world experience.

University of British Columbia

DIGGING UP THE TRUTH

Investigative journalism is a specialized type of news coverage. It involves in-depth research, organized information gathering, and **painstaking** fact-checking. Usually, the goal of investigative journalism is to raise public awareness about a social concern. It can also reveal abuse of power, criminal activity, or other important truths about the world.

Unlike daily news reporting, investigative journalism doesn't happen quickly. It can take months, or even years, for investigative journalists to pull together solid stories.

First, they need an idea. Sometimes, this happens accidentally. A reporter might stumble upon a secret document, overhear a private conversation, or discover **budget** numbers that don't add up. At other times, reporters begin investigating topics out of personal interest, from questions raised while researching previous news stories, or because of a hunch that something isn't quite right.

Once a journalist comes up with an idea, he or she starts researching. This is the time-consuming part of the process. Research might include interviewing people who have personal knowledge or experience in an area, studying documents and **data**, or reading media, **legal**, and other reports.

A DEFINITION AND AN EXPLANATION

The **United Nations** defines investigative journalism as "the unveiling of matters that are **concealed** either deliberately by someone in a position of power, or accidentally, behind a **chaotic** mass of facts and circumstances— and the analysis and exposure of all relevant facts to the public."

That means investigative journalists uncover hidden stories, research them, and report them to the public. These stories might be kept secret on purpose. Other times, the stories aren't deliberately hidden— they're just buried so deep in documents, data, and details that nobody has dug them up yet.

The United Nations is an international organization made up of 193 countries. Its goal is to maintain world peace and solve global issues.

During and after the research process, investigative journalists must **verify** every piece of information they receive or discover. That means double-checking data, confirming information through multiple sources, and **cross-checking** documents.

This is one of the most important elements in investigative journalism. Like a lawyer proving a case in **court**, the investigative journalist must be absolutely sure a story is true before presenting it to the public.

Investigative journalism projects take a lot of time and effort—and that costs money. Major newspapers, such as *The New York Times*, *The Boston Globe*, and *The Washington Post* can afford to have investigative departments. Many smaller media outlets can't. That's not to say they don't conduct investigative reporting. It's just not necessarily a full-time focus for them.

But it's not just the big newspapers and TV networks that produce investigative journalism projects. Today, a variety of independent journalists, **nonprofit** media foundations, and even university students, such as the UBC students who produced the e-waste documentary, specialize in this type of journalism.

They do it to make a difference in the world, to tell stories that need to be told, and to help right social wrongs.

WHAT IS THE DIFFERENCE?

Investigative journalism is defined in more than one way. However, most people agree that it differs from conventional reporting in a number of areas:

INVESTIGATIVE JOURNALISM

- Reporter is **proactive**, takes initiative to find original stories
- Project is long-term and requires in-depth research
- Goal of reporter is to question
- Stories expose issues surrounded in secrecy or silence
- Work often leads to social change

CONVENTIONAL JOURNALISM

- Reporter reacts to information provided by sources, such as police
- Projects are short-term, usually daily reporting, presenting news, events, and happenings of the day
- Goal of reporter is to inform
- Stories present the facts of the world as they are, without questioning

FOR THE PLANET

Almost any topic can be the subject of an investigative journalism project—including health, human rights, business, sports, and in the case of this book, environmental issues.

Reporters around the world pursue environmental investigative journalism stories about a variety of topics. In recent years, they have tackled such subjects as the environmental impact of the oil and gas industry, water pollution, and the loss of rain forests and wildlife habitat. Environmental stories are rarely about a single issue. Often, they are connected to business, financial, political, health, or human rights concerns.

THE STORY OF THE 5Ws

When a reporter presents a news story, he or she answers five basic questions—who, what, when, where, and why. Sometimes, journalists add an H—for how. Other times, the answers to the 5Ws take care of the H. Using the 5Ws, reporters tell different types of stories.

News stories are about the happenings of the day, such as a court case or a car accident. These are typically short and packed with facts.

Feature stories are longer reports that allow the journalist to provide more information, include more points of view, and dig deeper into a subject.

News features are a blend of news stories and feature stories. They are feature stories inspired by news events. For example, a news story about a flood would include the facts about the flood. A news feature might use the flood as a launching point to address how you might protect your home from damage in a future flood. A news feature is often the starting point for an investigative journalism piece.

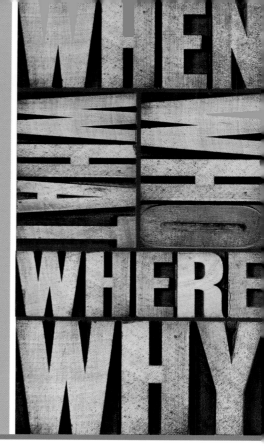

LEAKY JOURNALISM

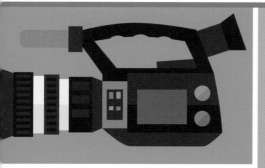

Sometimes a person in a position of knowledge "leaks" secret information to a journalist. That means he or she provides information without permission. Sometimes, just to grab headlines, a news outlet might publish the information without confirming that it's true. This can lead to problems for the person who provided the information, for the journalist, and for the people—or organizations—mentioned in the information.

Investigative journalism projects can sometimes begin with a leaked document. But before making the story public, the investigative journalist confirms that the leaked information is reliable, researches all related **angles** and background, analyzes information, and fact-checks every detail.

Environmental investigative journalists work to expose issues about the environment, such as ways that people may be unknowingly causing harmful pollution. They do not, however, actively push for change. They present the facts so that people can make their own decisions.

The goal of environmental investigative journalism is to educate the public about environmental concerns that affect people around the world—and close to home. But environmental journalists are not **activists**. They are not paid by environmental groups to do the work they do. Like most investigative journalists, they pursue these stories because of a personal curiosity, a passion for truth, and the desire to help Earth.

This book focuses on three specific environmental journalism investigations—a report about excessive water use by the wealthy, a piece about a chemical company that poisoned a community, and the e-waste documentary produced by the UBC students and their professor.

The group of reporters on the water story analyzed **satellite** images, used an **algorithm** to study drought, and examined landscape planning. The journalist who documented the poisoned community reviewed mountains of legal and government documents. And the UBC students conducted interviews through translators, went undercover, and crossed the globe to track e-waste. Their story started with a classroom assignment.

RULES THAT RULE

Journalists follow codes of ethics. These are sets of principles that outline acceptable and unacceptable behaviors for their work. They include commitments to such things as **integrity**, fairness, truth, and accuracy. Journalists also follow federal, state, or provincial laws relating to privacy and **copyright**.

increase
and which should
relate to this.
Copyright: the leg
and exclusive right
the intellectual prop

MEDIA MATTERS

Media is the plural form of the word medium. A medium is a method of mass communication, or a way to deliver information to a wide variety of people. Today, we receive news and information via a variety of media—newspapers, magazines, radio, TV, and the Internet.

All types of media are used to present investigative journalism stories, but each medium uses different techniques to reach its audience.

Newspapers and magazines deliver printed stories and photographs. An investigative journalist working in print media records and writes down interviews, and a photographer takes pictures to illustrate the story.

Radio shares messages using nothing but sound, so reporters in this medium focus on voices and audio recordings that allow the listener to hear the important elements of a story.

Some stories are so visually engaging that television or online video is the best medium to deliver the story. Video reporters record everything digitally or on videotape, then weave together on-camera interviews with video to present the story. Most video investigative projects are told in a long form called **documentary**, which is an in-depth look at a subject. *Ghana: Digital Dumping Ground* is a documentary that is about 20 minutes long.

Internet reporters use digital technology to present stories and documentaries in all of the formats mentioned above.

The type of media used to present a story can affect how readers or viewers engage with it or feel about it.

GHANA: DIGITAL DUMPING GROUND

WHO	E-waste industry
WHAT	Poisoning workers and the environment in developing countries; illegally accessing private information
WHEN	Discovered in 2008
WHERE	Ghana, China, India, and other nations
WHY	To make money
HOW	E-waste sent from North America to developing nations, where workers sort and burn e-waste in toxic dumps; criminals abuse or sell information obtained from old computers and phones

In 2008, University of British Columbia (UBC) Professor Peter Klein gave his International Reporting students an assignment. They were to produce a short documentary about a subject that affected people around the world. It also had to be a subject that had received little media coverage.

Sometimes, investigative journalism projects start with ideas that come to reporters from other people, from previous news stories, or from observing the world around them. In this case, an idea didn't come to the students—they had to go out and find one. To do this, they brainstormed with each other, asked questions of people in various occupations, and researched online.

In the end, the group of 10 **graduate students** chose to follow the trail of electronic waste, or e-waste. They wanted to know what happened to old computers, televisions, cell phones, and other electronics after consumers had delivered them to recycling centers.

Through their research, the students had found some evidence that the e-waste industry wasn't as eco-friendly as most people believed. What they discovered was worse than they had imagined. The e-waste trail took them to faraway nations, where toxic dumps were damaging the environment—and poisoning local citizens. They also discovered a link to international crime that grabbed the world's attention.

Programs such as the International Reporting Program (IRP) give journalism students valuable experience. They also provide a way to tell stories through investigative journalism.

UNIVERSITY NEWS GOES GLOBAL

Media budgets around the world are shrinking every year. Because of this, most newsrooms can no longer afford to dedicate the money and staff necessary to pursue investigative journalism projects. That means many important global issues are not being covered as fully as they should be.

To help cover some of those topics, Peter Klein founded the International Reporting Program (IRP) at the University of British Columbia in 2008. The student

program is funded by **grants,** sponsors, and donations.

Every year, IRP students work with experienced journalists to research, develop, and produce significant investigative journalism projects. Since it was founded, dozens of journalism students have traveled the world investigating and reporting on international stories.

Many of these stories have earned national and international awards, such as the three below.

The Pain Project (2011), a three-part documentary about people who suffer because they can't get painkillers, won two Canadian Online Publishing Awards.

Out of the Shadows (2015), a multimedia project about global mental health, earned three Canadian journalism awards and one international honor.

China's Generation Green (2014), about China's environmental crisis and the individuals working to change it, won four Canadian national news awards.

FROM WEST TO EAST

Like all investigative journalists, the UBC students approached their e-waste story with a step-by-step plan.

They started with a trip to a recycling depot in Vancouver, BC. There, they dropped off a few old computer monitors for recycling. They wore hidden cameras to record the visit to the facility. The worker who took their e-waste assured them the monitors would be disposed of completely, safely, and locally. This usually means that the waste wouldn't be sent to another country or continent.

The students wanted to know if this was, in fact, what would happen to their discarded devices.

Because the goal of their investigative project was to follow the e-waste trail from start to finish, they waited to see what would happen to their equipment. "We watched it get put into a shipping container, wrote down the number of the container, and tracked it online," said Professor Peter Klein.

Public records often provide good starting points for investigative journalism projects. They contain vast amounts of information that often lead to surprising discoveries.

In this case, Peter and his students used online records to follow their e-waste. They were surprised to learn that the container holding their computers was headed for Hong Kong, a **territory** of China. That's 6,400 miles (10,300 km) from Vancouver.

At some recycling facilities, e-waste is stored in bins such as these before being sorted into shipping containers like the blue ones behind the bins.

Just as investigative journalists would, the students tracked multiple shipping containers across the globe to prove that their suspicions—that e-waste was not recycled locally—were true.

At the recycling yard, the students had noted the numbers of other e-waste-filled containers. Online tracking showed that these, too, were headed for Asia. Despite what they had been told, e-waste was not being processed locally. "It turned out the e-waste was ending up in dumps all over the world," said Peter. To confirm this, Peter and some of the students flew to Hong Kong.

Investigative journalists must check and double-check every element of a story before presenting it to the public. They can't rely on a single source—such as online records—to prove something is true.

In this case, Peter and the students had to confirm that the shipping containers ended up in Asia as the online tracking indicated they would. The only way to do that was to see for themselves. Once in Hong Kong, they witnessed the arrival of stacks of shipping containers filled with old computers, printers, phones, and other devices.

"We [saw] for ourselves how hundreds of millions of tons of old electronics are slipped out of North America," said Peter in the documentary. From there, he added, the electronics end up in illegal **markets**, where they are bought and sold, on the other side of the world.

The group knew they had to continue following the e-waste trail to confirm what their research had suggested. They decided to travel to a small Chinese town called Guiyu, which they heard was a center of e-waste disposal.

What they discovered in Guiyu was shocking. There were miles and miles of old electronics in the town, Peter describes. He and his students learned that almost everyone in the town worked in the e-waste industry. Workers earned bits of money, but paid a huge price in terms of their health.

In Guiyu, the group watched workers "cook" circuit boards to extract tiny amounts of precious metals to sell.

Circuit boards contain toxic chemicals. As the boards melt, the workers inhale the smoky fumes, slowly poisoning themselves.

Meanwhile, they saw small children searching e-waste dumps to find anything they could use or sell. At the dumps, the e-waste is set on fire at burn sites to melt plastic and rubber casings, leaving behind valuable bits of copper wire and other metals. When searching these burn sites, the children cut themselves on metal, glass, and sharp plastic from broken electronic leftovers. They also inhale deadly smoke.

Guiyu is the dirty little secret of the high-tech industry. The workers have no idea of the long-term impacts to their children. They don't realize what's really happening to their health.

Jim Puckett, American environmental activist, interviewed for the UBC documentary

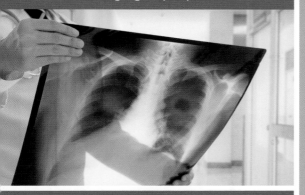
The heavy metals found in electronics can be damaging to people's health.

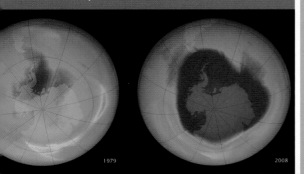
Earth's ozone layer has been damaged over the years. The purple circle shows a large hole in the year 2008, which was not present in 1979.

1979   2008

HARMFUL TO HUMANS AND THE ENVIRONMENT

Electronic devices contain dozens of different materials and chemicals. Many of these compounds are toxic to people and the environment.

Heavy metals, such as lead, cadmium, and mercury, are common in computer and TV screens and batteries. In the human body, these metals can damage **organ** functions and the systems the body relies on to work, such as the **nervous system**. Some of these chemicals can cause cancer. All of these chemicals have a stronger impact on children because their bodies are small and still growing.

The chemicals and materials in e-waste also harm the environment. Certain plastics, for example, don't break down easily, meaning they stay in—and pollute—water and soil for a long time. Others enter the atmosphere and damage Earth's ozone layer. The ozone layer is the part of the atmosphere that protects the planet from the Sun's harmful **radiation**.

As part of their work, investigative journalists might search for trends or seek to discover how many people are affected by a particular problem. Again, they must provide concrete evidence before reporting these things to the public. To confirm facts, journalists might study documents, conduct interviews with a variety of people, or witness—and film—the situation for themselves.

These reporters, for example, couldn't say that e-waste disposal was an international concern without verifying it. So while Peter Klein and one group of students followed the e-waste trail through China, two other groups investigated the e-waste situations in Ghana and India.

The team witnessed similar horrific e-waste dumps in every region they visited. In addition to the health problems created by this dangerous business, the environment also suffered. Dead rivers, air pollution, and charred landscapes are a few of the eco-hazards the students witnessed.

THE STORY TAKES A TWIST

One of the first rules of journalism is to be open to wherever an investigation happens to take you. Reporters have no idea what their research might uncover.

In the case of the e-waste investigation, the trio of UBC students assigned to Ghana accidentally uncovered a whole other side to the story—an angle that ended up almost taking the focus off the environmental and health impacts of e-waste disposal. That group started its trip at a place called Agbogbloshie, near Accra, the largest city in Ghana. They had heard Agbogbloshie was the site of one of the world's most sickening toxic e-waste dumps—and that's exactly what they found there.

Once a beautiful wetland area full of birds, fish, and wildlife, this part of Agbogbloshie had become one of the most polluted places on Earth. The river bubbled with black and green toxic waste. The smelly air was full of pollution, and the ground was scorched and covered with garbage. The reporters witnessed people living in **slums**.

In Agbogbloshie, the reporters also discovered an unexpected criminal connection to the e-waste story. They learned the old computers and hard drives that still worked were being bought and sold in public markets. People who couldn't afford to buy new equipment often bought secondhand parts in these markets. However, criminals also bought them because the hard drives often contained the original owners' information—photographs, credit card numbers, financial details, and more.

The students in Ghana witnessed something similar to those in Guiyu: children searching toxic dumps for electronics to burn and sell.

The investigation took a new direction when the students discovered only about half of the e-waste was being burned in dumps (above). They followed the trail to find out what happened to the unburned e-waste.

Journalists are trained to recognize important stories when they see them. In this case, the UBC students realized they had just discovered another major angle to the e-waste story—one that would impact people around the globe and had criminal consequences.

They immediately switched their focus to follow this new lead. They needed to know whether it was true that criminals could get personal information from e-waste sold in the public markets. To do so, one of the students bought five hard drives at a public market for about $35 each. Another student filmed her making the purchase, using a hidden camera.

Since criminal activity was involved, they did not want others to know they were investigating this lead.

The students brought the hard drives to a computer scientist, who analyzed them. Within minutes, he had accessed all kinds of private details the previous owners may not have even known were there. Surprisingly, the information was easy to find and access. No special skills or computer programs were needed to read it.

Criminals can use this information to steal money from bank accounts, conduct online and telephone scams, and even to **blackmail** the computers' previous owners.

Video journalism is a way for reporters to show viewers evidence of the things they witnessed.

"The flow of electronic waste from the western world to the developing world is a very, very important story. Companies here in Canada will say, 'Yeah, we're going to recycle your broken or used electronics locally and safely,' and then they put it into a shipping container and ship it to Hong Kong."

Blake Sifton, former UBC grad student, in *Maclean's* magazine, 2009

CHANGE-MAKING JOURNALISM

After five months of traveling, interviewing, hidden-camera recording, researching, and note-taking, Professor Klein and his students packaged their findings into a 20-minute documentary entitled *Ghana: Digital Dumping Ground*. The film aired on a major American TV news magazine called *Frontline* in June 2009.

Immediately, the U.S. government tightened its rules relating to exporting, or sending, e-waste to other countries. The story was also picked up and covered by a number of other media outlets, generating much public outrage.

Most of the attention the film drew was related to the criminal element of the story. For the students, however, that wasn't the main point of the documentary. For them, revealing the harm caused by the toxic e-waste dumps was the goal.

Since then, the e-waste dump at Guiyu has been cleaned up, but the situation in Ghana and India remains mostly unchanged.

Still, said Professor Peter Klein, now that the public knows about e-waste dumps and the harm they cause, companies are under more pressure to make sure they dispose of e-waste safely and responsibly.

Corporations in many American states and Canadian provinces, for example, must follow e-waste recycling laws. There are public and government programs that certify these corporations as responsible recyclers of e-waste.

Certified companies agree to follow requirements related to e-waste disposal. Among other things, they make sure the materials they dispose are not harmful, and they protect the safety of the workers who will be exposed to the materials.

Today, the students who produced the e-waste documentary are working around the world. They are based in Canada, the United States, Africa, the Middle East, and the South Pacific. They work in a variety of roles for a variety of media.

In 2010, the students' documentary won an Emmy Award. It also won a prize for best documentary of the year from the Society for Professional Journalists.

PETER W KLEIN

Ghana: Digital Dumping Ground

WATCH VIDEO ▶
Airs Tuesday, June 23, 2009, at 9:00 p.m. ET on PBS
GHANA: DIGITAL DUMPING GROUND
As this month's digital television conversion makes tens of millions of analog TVs obsolete, and Americans continue to trash computers and cell phones at alarming rates, FRONTLINE/World presents a global investigation into the dirty secret of the digital age — the dumping and dangerous recycling of hundreds of millions of pounds of electronic waste across the developing world. The report also uncovers another byproduct of our disposable culture - data fraud, as thousands of old hard drives are finding their way into criminal hands. Read More ▶

IT TAKES A TEAM

Ghana: Digital Dumping Ground is a television documentary. The documentary is a common way to present investigative journalism projects. But documentaries tend to be more labor intensive—meaning their production involves more people—than a written investigative journalism story.

Like written stories, documentaries require reporters to research and tell the stories. Written stories usually involve a photographer, who adds images to the story; editors, who fine-tune the story; and **graphic designers**, who add visual elements to the text.

A TV team needs all those people, and several more. A producer oversees the whole project. Videographers—often more than one—record interviews and collect video images of every aspect of a story. This includes such things as the location of a story, the people in that location, and anything mentioned in the story. For example, in *Ghana: Digital Dumping Ground*, the videographers captured images of children working in e-waste dumps in different nations.

Sometimes, video crews also include people who specialize in sound and lighting.

After the videographers and reporters have gathered information, a video editor works with the team to organize the images and interviews into a logical story. A scriptwriter (who may also be the reporter) writes a script for the reporter to read into a microphone. The script is used to link together the visual elements of the story.

Before a story is ready to be seen on television, it may also require music, animation, and special effects. Different people usually perform each of these different tasks—making a documentary a team effort.

The students recorded interviews with people who were willing to talk about the e-waste industry. These interviews were featured in the documentary.

21

"THE WET PRINCE OF BEL AIR"

WHO	Wealthy homeowners
WHAT	Abused a limited **natural resource**
WHEN	2014–2015
WHERE	Los Angeles and other cities in California
WHY	To maintain beautiful gardens, swimming pools, and healthy landscaping
HOW	By wasting millions of gallons of water during a drought

Many environmental issues have an impact on the entire planet—but they also affect humanity at a local level. E-waste, **climate change**, and **habitat** loss are examples of issues that touch everyone on the planet.

It's impossible for an investigative journalist to study how an issue affects every person on Earth. So sometimes, they address global issues by focusing on a specific problem in a specific place.

That was the case with a group of reporters who worked for the Center for Investigative Reporting in Emeryville, California. In 2015, they discovered that wealthy homeowners in their state were wasting millions of gallons of water in a time of severe drought.

A drought is a period of unusually dry weather, with little rainfall to fill lakes, rivers, and other bodies of water. Every living thing needs water to survive, so droughts can lead to shortages of drinking water, damage to plant and animal life, and the loss of crops on farms.

The availability of clean water is a worldwide concern. So is drought. In this case, the reporters looked no farther than their own backyards—or, more accurately, at their neighbors' backyards—to find an important story.

> Virtually all aspects of environmental stories are local. [...] But these stories are also unfailingly global—a local environmental issue is almost certainly **replicated** in many other places around the world.
>
> **J-Source: The Canadian Journalism Project**

WATER FOR THE WEALTHY

Like many good investigative journalism pieces, this one stemmed from one of the qualities shared by all good investigative journalists—plain, old-fashioned curiosity.

In 2015, California was in the midst of its worst drought in **recorded history**. City governments encouraged residents to curb their water use. Some imposed watering restrictions and fines for violating, or breaking, those restrictions. Others only allowed homeowners to water their lawns or wash their cars on certain days of the week. In many towns, allowing water to drain into the street was a no-no. Some areas even limited toilet flushing.

Despite these rules, as reporters Lance Williams, Katharine Mieszkowski, and Michael Corey noticed, many large California estates still had gorgeous green lawns, full swimming pools, fountains, and thriving gardens. The reporters knew that such beautiful surroundings required water, and lots of it. They wondered how these residences could maintain such lush lawns and gardens in a time of water restrictions. They wanted to know who was wasting the region's precious natural resource.

The California drought lasted from 2012 to 2016. California residents are still encouraged to conserve water.

The reporters started their research by reviewing public utility records. Public utilities are businesses that provide necessary services to a community, such as water, electricity, natural gas, and telephone. Public records, such as records that show the amount of utilities people use, are a common starting point for investigative journalism.

The reporters were shocked by what they found in the utility records. The paperwork showed that 365 California residences had each used more than 1 million gallons (3.8 million liters) of water in the previous year. That's eight families' worth of water each. The worst offender used "an astonishing 11.8 million gallons (44.7 million liters) of water in one year—enough for 90 households."

The reporters were shocked to learn that a Los Angeles resident could be fined for washing a car on the wrong day of the week—but there were no limits on the amount of water a single homeowner there could use.

The reporters' research showed that 92 of California's top 100 water-wasting homes were located in wealthy neighborhoods and small cities in Los Angeles County, such as Beverly Hills (below).

Armed with this information, the journalists approached 22 different public utility companies around the state. These are the organizations that monitor and bill residents for water use. The public records had revealed the zip codes of the water mega-users—but the reporters wanted names. They wanted to talk to the homeowners who were ignoring the drought. None of the public agencies they approached would hand over those details. Some said **privacy laws** forbade them to give out that information. Others said they didn't track water consumption.

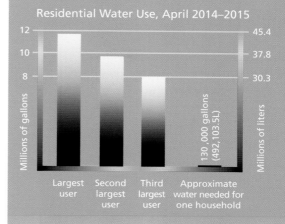

This chart, created according to the reporters' data, shows the stark difference between the amount of water used by the three highest users, and the approximate amount needed for one household.

PUBLIC OR PRIVATE?

More than 100 countries around the world have Freedom of Information (FOI) laws. Under these laws, citizens can request access to government documents. The goal is to prevent governments from keeping secrets from their citizens.

Anyone can request and receive government information—including paper documents, photographs, videos, e-mails, and databases. However, there are cases in which requests are denied.

In some cases, government records are incomplete, meaning certain documents simply don't exist. Sometimes, finding and delivering the requested documents can take months, or even years.

In many countries, including the United States and Canada, there are also exceptions to FOI laws. That means, in certain situations, governments don't have to hand over information. For example, they can refuse to release information that could threaten national security, break laws, or invade a person's privacy.

Investigative journalists often request information under FOI laws to help with their research. If their requests are denied, the journalists, like all citizens, have the right to challenge the decision in court. Journalists often argue that the public's right to know is more important than the government's right to keep secrets from its citizens. In such cases, it's up to individual judges to make the final decisions.

GOING PUBLIC

The three reporters believed the public had a right to know about the water abuse by the wealthy. They didn't have all the details they wanted, but they had enough to produce a story. They published it on *Reveal*, the online platform where the Center for Investigative Reporting presents its work.

The story, entitled "The Wet Prince of Bel Air: Who Is California's Biggest Water Guzzler?" ran in October 2015.

In it, the journalists documented their research process, their discoveries, and a summary of the state's worst water abusers. They named Los Angeles, the San Francisco Bay Area, and San Diego as the places where the state's top water wasters lived. They also pinpointed the posh neighborhoods that wasted the most H_2O.

The trio of journalists knew there was more to the story, though. They refused to give up on it— as did their outraged readers.

Immediately after Reveal *published the "Wet Prince" story, four Los Angeles city councilors proposed finding and penalizing the city's major water wasters. The proposal did not pass, however.*

Read ▼   Listen   Watch

Reveal

from The Center for Investigative Reporting

About Us   Donate

The Secrets of the Drought

Hidden stories from California's historic drought

SUSTAINABILITY / **THE SECRETS OF THE DROUGHT**

THE SECRETS OF THE DROUGHT

Who is the Wet Prince of Bel Air? Here are the likely culprits

Los Angeles officials have steadfastly refused to identify the Wet Prince of Bel Air, the homeowner who pumped an astonishing 11.8 million gallons of water during a single year of California's crippling drought. So we decided to figure it out ourselves. The hard way.

CLIMATE CHANGE

This California lawmaker wants to name and shame 'The Wet Princes'

State Sen. Jerry Hill wants California to smack its biggest water users with hefty fines and bad publicity.

THE SECRETS OF THE DROUGHT

California cracks down on its Wet Princes

California will crack down on future "Wet Princes" – homeowners who use enormous quantities of water during droughts.

THE INVESTIGATION CONTINUES—WITH A LITTLE HELP

The "Wet Prince" story was successful, but Lance, Katharine, and Michael wanted to find more details that would help pinpoint the water-wasting homes.

Investigative journalists often have to be inventive in their research. If the information they want isn't available through obvious methods, they often come up with other ways to find it. In this case, the reporters were helped by community members and other citizens who were interested in finding the water wasters, too.

A columnist for the *LA Times* newspaper made it his mission to find and name the waster who had used the most water the previous year. A group of private citizens did the same. They all failed to find the offending home.

A graduate student at the University of Oklahoma also reacted to the "Wet Prince" story. He sent an e-mail to the *Reveal* journalists, suggesting that they use satellite images to track down the over-the-top water users.

Thanks to the graduate student's idea, the reporters turned to technology. With a team of data analysts, they created a scientific process for identifying the water-hogging Los Angeles homes.

> Investigative reporting is all about checking things twice. First to see what's going on, and then second to source it. "

**Lance Williams,
senior reporter, *Reveal***

A scientific process is a way of using science to make observations and answer questions. It usually involves making predictions and carrying out experiments. Investigative journalists sometimes use or create their own scientific process to answer questions about an issue.

They started with **aerial** photographs and real estate maps to identify homes with lush green properties, a sure sign of heavy water use. Next, they used an algorithm to narrow down the residences with the healthiest plant life.

Because investigative journalists must check and double-check their facts, these reporters used a second technique to verify the first set of their findings. This time they analyzed satellite imagery using a technique developed by the National Aeronautics and Space Administration (NASA). This allowed them to track moisture levels in the soil—from space! High moisture content in the soil meant heavy watering on the ground.

Still, that wasn't enough proof for these investigative journalists. Environmental reporters often turn to science to find evidence to support their ideas or theories. And science is never simple.

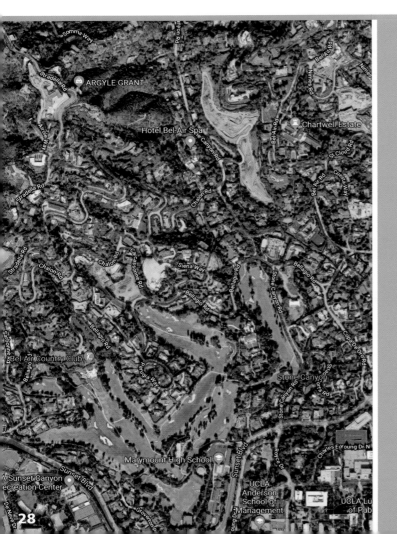

DRIVEN BY DATA

In the past, a journalist's job mostly involved seeking out information. They would do this by interviewing people, reading, researching, and observing activities and events. Today, because information is everywhere online, the journalist's job has changed.

Now, in addition to finding information, journalists must process the vast amounts of information they find. That's where the help from data analysts comes in.

Any information can be considered data—it isn't just numbers. Data analysts help journalists find data, organize it, and understand what it means.

Analyzing data can lead to new story ideas, discovering hidden connections between powerful people, or finding new ways to answer questions—just as the reporters on the "Wet Prince" stories did.

In this case, moist soil didn't necessarily prove that homeowners overwatered their properties. That's because different plants need different amounts of water to stay healthy. Some need water every day, while others can go for a week between sprinklings.

The reporters turned to landscaping experts to find out which plants guzzle the most moisture. They learned that grass, and certain trees and shrubs, are the thirstiest.

Next, they measured property sizes and applied a mathematical formula to figure out which homes had the most of these particular plants. These would be the properties that needed the most water.

The keys to good investigative journalism are research and verification, or confirmation, that all facts and figures are correct. To triple-check their findings, the *Reveal* reporters asked three different experts to review their measurements, and math, data, and scientific processes. "They all said what we did checked out," wrote Michael.

The investigation took a year of scientific research, **data mining**, calculations, and fact-checking. Finally, the reporters were able to identify the Los Angeles properties they believed used the most water.

In the fall of 2016, they published two more stories on the *Reveal* website, detailing their findings and describing their investigative techniques.

CHANGE-MAKING JOURNALISM

In January 2017, *Reveal* published the fourth and final installment in its water-abuse series. This article summarized the previous stories, and reported on the impact the journalists' investigation had on the community.

They reported that, in the year after the initial story, the worst of the water abusers had cut their total water use by 12 percent. The largest amount of water used by a single home dropped from 11.8 to 9.8 million gallons (44.7 to 37.1 million liters) a year.

Meanwhile, city officials had contacted each of the original mega water users and asked them to cut back. Most homeowners said they hadn't realized they'd been hogging the water. They agreed to reduce their use. Forty-five of the top 100 users in the city cut their excessive watering by so much during the following year that they were no longer on the top-100 list.

Since then, the city of Los Angeles has also changed the way it bills water users. Now, as soon as a residence's use hits a certain level, the price per gallon goes up.

QUALITIES OF AN INVESTIGATIVE JOURNALIST

Investigative journalists work in different types of media, focus on different subject areas, and live in different parts of the world. Despite these differences, they all have a few things in common. Good investigative reporters excel at their work because they possess certain personal qualities:

CURIOSITY	They ask questions about how the world works.
INITIATIVE	They know how to spot good stories and find stories other reporters aren't covering.
RESEARCH SKILLS	They know where to find information.
DEDICATION AND PATIENCE	They're willing to wait. It often takes months or years to gather all the information needed to fully tell a story; sometimes, they wait weeks or months to access a single document or to get a reply from a government body or other source.
FLEXIBILITY	They may have to change direction mid-investigation.
LOGIC AND ORGANIZATION	They conduct step-by-step investigations, manage massive amounts of information, and arrange that information into easy-to-understand stories.
ETHICS	They respect their sources, follow rules and laws about such things as privacy, and verify all the facts before making a story public.
COURAGE	They stay strong in the face of criticism and threats of violence or legal action, which occur just because they're doing their jobs and revealing truths that others want hidden.

Customers can be fined up to $40,000 for "unreasonable use" under the new system.

The state of California also made a change because of the public outrage that followed the "Wet Prince" stories. It is now against the law to use excessive water during times of drought emergencies. Anyone breaking that law can be heavily fined.

For the *Reveal* reporters—Lance Williams, Katharine Mieszkowski, and Michael Corey—the "Wet Prince of Bel Air" series was a triumph of investigative journalism.

Media outlets from Los Angeles to New York City followed up on the story. Even a major newspaper in England covered it, drawing international attention to the water-abuse issue.

In addition, the trio's four-part series earned one of the world's most important and respected awards for environmental journalism. The Society of Environmental Journalists presented the reporters with the 2016 Award for Outstanding In-Depth Environmental Reporting.

All three reporters still work for the Center for Investigative Reporting.

A powerful combination of traditional shoe-leather reporting and cutting-edge data mining, this compellingly written series is an inspiring example for other journalists to not take 'no' for an answer when public officials hide behind a **restrictive** interpretation of public records laws.

Judge's comments about "The Wet Prince of Bel Air" series, in awarding it the Society of Environmental Journalists' top prize, 2016

DUPONT INVESTIGATION

WHO	DuPont, an American science and engineering company
WHAT	Poisoned workers, animals, drinking water, soil
WHEN	1948–2015
WHERE	Parkersburg, West Virginia, and surrounding areas
WHY	To make money
HOW	By knowingly using a toxic chemical in its products

In 2014, reporter Mariah Blake finished up a major investigative piece on toxic plastics. Next, she planned to write a book about laws and regulations that control the plastics industry.

Early in her research, however, she stumbled on a set of legal documents that took her in a whole new direction. One quality of a good investigative journalist is the ability to spot a good story and run with it. Even though Mariah had started with a different idea, she immediately shifted her focus to this new one.

What she discovered was, about 10 years earlier, a group of 80,000 people had sued a huge company called DuPont. The people all had suffered health problems caused by a chemical named C8. DuPont had used this chemical at its factory in West Virginia. One of the products the factory made was Teflon, a nonstick coating for pots and pans.

But it wasn't just factory workers who'd been ill. Because DuPont had released the chemical into the water and air, C8 had poisoned people for miles around. That's why the **lawsuit** had involved so many individuals.

What was worse, as Mariah discovered, was that DuPont executives had known C8 was harmful to humans and animals, and they had continued to use it anyway—for more than 50 years. That's why the people won their lawsuit.

WHAT IS C8?

C8 is short for perfluorooctanoic acid. This is a chemical that "makes things slippery and stainproof," said journalist Mariah Blake.

The substance was developed in the 1940s. Scientists started studying it in the early 1960s, because some people feared C8 was harming their health. Studies have since linked C8 to a number of diseases, including certain cancers, internal bleeding, and birth defects.

C8 was manufactured by a company called 3M and used in products made by eight other companies, including DuPont. When 3M discovered C8 was harmful, it stopped producing it. So, DuPont started making it.

Not only is C8 toxic, but it doesn't break down in the environment. Today, it is found, literally, everywhere on Earth—and in almost every human and animal body on the planet. "It will be here for probably thousands of years," said Mariah.

Companies, including DuPont, have now stopped using C8. But they have replaced it with chemicals that are very similar. The side effects, or consequences, of these substances are not yet known.

DuPont is a huge company that was founded in 1802 to make gunpowder. Today, it is known as DowDuPont and makes a variety of products, such as plastics, protective fabrics, Styrofoam parts for electronic devices, chemicals, and glues. It also makes products for farming, such as pesticides (which kill bugs) and fast-growing seeds.

WHERE WAS C8 USED?

Until it was phased out in 2015, DuPont used C8 in a number of its products, including Teflon, a nonstick coating for pots and pans. DuPont and seven other companies used it in such common items as clumping kitty litter, dental floss, floor polish, wax paper, firefighting foam, outdoor clothing, carpets, and cosmetics. It is no longer used in these products.

LEGAL LEGWORK

DuPont workers had first raised concerns about C8's safety in the 1950s. The company insisted the chemical was "safe as soap" to handle. At the time, DuPont had assured the surrounding community that, even though the local water contained a tiny bit of C8, it was still perfectly fine to drink. Area residents—many of whom worked at DuPont—took the company's word for it.

Meanwhile, starting in 1961, DuPont conducted a series of secret studies that proved C8 was harmful. Instead of protecting workers and local residents, the company hid the study results. DuPont continued to use C8, meaning it had knowingly poisoned thousands of people, animals, and the environment.

The truth about C8 started to emerge in 1999, when a local West Virginia farmer and his wife hired a lawyer to sue DuPont. The farmer's cattle had been dying horrible deaths at an alarming rate. He blamed DuPont and its nearby waste dump for killing the herd.

During court proceedings, a judge forced DuPont to hand thousands of internal documents over to the couple's lawyer, Rob Bilott. In that mass of paperwork, Rob discovered the truth about DuPont and C8. "It became apparent what was going on," he said in a 2016 *The New York Times* article. "DuPont had for decades been actively trying to conceal their actions. They knew this stuff was harmful, and they put it in the water anyway."

In 2001, DuPont paid the farmer to cover the cost of the cattle he had lost. That meant the lawsuit was over—but Rob didn't stop there. He knew there was more to this story. He reported DuPont to the Environmental Protection Agency (EPA).

Around the same time, another local resident hired Rob's law firm to sue DuPont over its use of C8. Ultimately, 80,000 people joined this man's fight. They filed a class action lawsuit, meaning they all got together to sue DuPont.

In 2003, because of the evidence the lawyers presented, a judge ruled that C8 was "toxic." Two years later, DuPont settled, or resolved, the class action lawsuit. The company agreed to clean up local waterways and create a health and education fund for those affected by C8.

In 2004, the EPA sued DuPont for deliberately hiding evidence that proved C8 was toxic. In 2006, DuPont paid the EPA a $16.5-million fine.

Despite all this legal action, the chemical company continued to earn more than $1 billion a year from products containing C8. Surprisingly, it was never ordered to stop using the poisonous chemical.

DuPont voluntarily stopped using C8 in its products in 2015. This was more than 10 years after the chemical was proven—in court— to be toxic, and linked to a variety of cancers and other diseases.

The U.S. Environmental Protection Agency (EPA) protects human health and the environment. Among other things, it makes sure people follow laws that protect health and the environment, researches environmental and health-related issues, and educates the public about these issues.

William Jefferson Clinton Federal Building

12th Street, NW Entrance

U.S. Environmental Protection Agency

(North and South Entrances)

TIMELINE

1951 DuPont begins using C8 in Teflon products at its factory in West Virginia.

1961 Researchers at DuPont confirm that C8 is toxic.

1978 DuPont learns that C8 is building up in their workers' blood, causing health issues.

1984 DuPont monitors local West Virginia drinking water; later finds C8 contamination.

1999 The local farmer, whose animals had been dying, sues DuPont.

2000 3M stops making C8. DuPont later begins making its own.

2001 DuPont pays the farmer; class action lawsuit is filed against DuPont.

2005 DuPont settles class action lawsuit, is fined by EPA for hiding evidence that C8 was toxic.

2015 DuPont voluntarily stops using C8.

ENTER THE INVESTIGATIVE JOURNALIST

By the time Mariah Blake came across the DuPont and C8 story in 2014, all of these events were ancient history. Plus, because of lawyer Rob Bilott's 16-year mission to uncover the truth about DuPont, all the documents relating to the class action and EPA lawsuits were in the public record.

The story was no secret. So why hadn't Mariah—or anyone else—heard about it?

"This was a decades-long **conspiracy** to cover up the health effects of this chemical, but it really hadn't gotten much attention," said Mariah in a 2015 radio interview.

Not only were the facts buried in stacks of legal documents, but DuPont had done everything it could to keep the story out of the public eye.

Mariah felt the public had a right to know about C8 and DuPont's efforts to hide the information. She also suspected there was more to the story yet to be uncovered.

Research is the first step in any investigative journalism project. Mariah started her research by going through the information that was already available—the thousands of pages of documents lawyers had discovered a decade earlier.

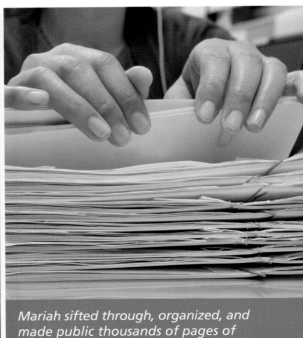

Mariah sifted through, organized, and made public thousands of pages of documents that previously had been difficult to find and understand.

She studied private memos, e-mails and letters, even diagrams and charts.

Using information from these documents, she pieced together a timeline of the DuPont story. She put together clear answers to the following questions and more: When did workers first express concerns about C8? When did DuPont scientists first discover the truth about the toxic chemical? When did lawyers get involved?

In the paperwork, she also discovered how far DuPont had gone to conceal evidence that C8 was poisonous.

In these documents, Mariah found potential sources, people who'd been affected by C8. She hoped to interview some of these individuals, to add a personal side to the story. Finding witnesses and others willing to speak out is important in investigative reporting.

At the time, about 3,500 individuals were still in the process of suing DuPont. These cases were still before the courts, so none of these people could speak to a reporter. Other potential sources were too sick. Many were dead.

Some people didn't want to talk to Mariah because they worried about how their friends and neighbors would react. Many people in the area still worked for DuPont. They were loyal to the company, despite the harm it had caused the community.

Investigative journalists are skilled at anticipating and answering questions that the public may have. As she began her investigation, Mariah asked all of the questions she knew the public would want answered.

Though it can sometimes be difficult to find sources willing to talk to journalists, interviewing the people involved in a story is an important part of an investigative journalism project.

DEDICATION AND DIGGING

Dedication is an important quality of investigative journalists. Mariah displayed that over the next five months. She didn't give up her search for information and for people who might speak to her.

Eventually, through off-the-record conversations, she learned there were more DuPont documents available—documents the lawyers had never seen. These papers had been part of the EPA lawsuit against DuPont. Some were available online, but most were buried in a library of EPA records in Washington, DC.

Mariah spent days there going through files.

A woman who had worked at the library for many years helped her sort through masses of paperwork. "It was only because she had a recollection of the case, from having been there for a long time, that she was able to find the documents," said Mariah. Sometimes, little coincidences like this are just what investigative journalists need to open doors to new information.

Thanks to the newly discovered paperwork, and eventually finding people willing to be interviewed,

Mariah finally had what she needed to pull together her news story.

Even though her research added new details and new voices to the C8 story, she credited Rob Bilott and his team of lawyers for doing most of the work. "They spent 16 years piecing together this story out of millions of pages of documents," she said in a 2015 interview. Because of their efforts, the information was there for a journalist to find.

So, if the details had been available for 10 years, why had nobody told the C8 story before? Mostly, it's because nobody other than those lawyers had ever taken the time to sift through the masses of paperwork. It was also because DuPont did everything it could to hide the truth—even after it had lost many lawsuits.

It took an investigative journalist like Mariah Blake to stumble upon the story, recognize its importance, and do the work to make it public. Her seven-chapter project appeared on the *Huffington Post*'s online magazine, *Highline*, in late-August 2015. "Welcome to Beautiful Parkersburg, West Virginia" featured text, photographs, video, and audio sections.

OFF-THE-RECORD

Sometimes, people know information that could help a journalist, but they do not want to be interviewed. There are many reasons for this. Often, people fear what might happen if others find out they have provided information. If the information is a company secret, for example, a person could be fired for revealing it. If the information involves government documents, a person could be punished for sharing it—even if it exposes government wrongdoing. If the information involves criminal activity, a person may risk physical harm or jail time for spilling the beans. Other times, a person simply fears that choosing to speak with a journalist will cause others to treat them differently.

In some of these situations, these individuals, also called sources, may be willing to talk to a journalist "off-the-record." This usually means that the source allows the journalist to publish the information, without revealing their name. But sometimes, "off-the-record" means that the journalist is not allowed to publish the source's name or the information. The source provides information for background only.

Journalists who have not been allowed to publish "off-the-record" information are challenged to verify those facts a different way.

> They didn't put the pieces together until there was a headline saying, 'This chemical may be toxic.' Then all of a sudden, the whole picture came into focus for them. All kinds of people suddenly realized this was the cause of their suffering.
>
> **Mariah Blake**

CHANGE-MAKING JOURNALISM

Coincidentally, while Mariah was researching C8 and DuPont, another investigative journalist was doing exactly the same thing. New York-based reporter Sharon Lerner published a three-part series on DuPont and C8 earlier in August 2015. "The Teflon Toxin" appeared in *The Intercept*, an independent, online publication dedicated to investigative journalism.

Like Mariah, Sharon had spent months going through the original legal documents. Like Mariah, she also uncovered new information during her research. Independently, but at the same time, these two investigative journalists made public something that had been hidden for decades.

Even many people affected by C8 had never linked their illnesses to DuPont. The articles helped them realize that the chemical was the cause of their suffering.

The social dynamics in the affected communities changed because of the articles, Mariah said. The residents who had first sued DuPont had been treated badly by other community members for years. Suddenly, those people were seen as heroes for standing up to the corporation.

The Intercept_

The Teflon Toxin

In this series, Sharon Lerner exposes DuPont's multi-decade cover-up of the severe harms to health associated with a chemical known as PFOA, or C8, and associated compounds such as PFOS and GenX.

PART 16
PFOA and PFOS Are Only the Best-Known Members of a Very Dangerous Class of Chemicals

PART 15
The U.S. Military Is Spending Millions to Replace Toxic Firefighting Foam with Toxic Firefighting Foam

PART 14
EPA Orders Testing for GenX Contamination Near Chemours Plant in West Virginia

PART 13
Citizen Groups Will Sue DuPont and Chemours for Contaminating Drinking Water in North Carolina

PART 12
New Teflon Toxin Found in North Carolina Drinking Water

PART 11
The Teflon Toxin Goes to China

PART 10
DuPont May Dodge Toxic Lawsuits By Pulling a Disappearing Act

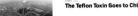

Mariah's and Sharon's articles raised awareness about C8 across the country and around the world.

For their work, Mariah and Sharon were nominated for the same National Magazine Award in 2016. Neither won, but Mariah's piece earned third place in the World Press Photo's 2016 Multimedia Contest for **Immersive** Storytelling.

Both reporters continue to work as investigative journalists. Mariah is a freelance reporter who covers a variety of topics. Sharon still works for *The Intercept*, focusing on stories about toxins in the environment.

Sharon is also featured in a documentary about the DuPont cover-up, entitled *The Devil We Know*. It premiered at the Sundance Film Festival in January 2018. Lawyer Rob Bilott is in the film, too.

In 2016, the *The New York Times* published a lengthy piece about Rob, entitled "The Lawyer Who Became DuPont's Worst Nightmare." In 2017, he earned the Right Livelihood Award. This is an international honor given to courageous people who tackle, and help solve, global problems.

CONCLUSION

Whether their work focuses on the environment, human rights, health, sports, or other topics, all investigative journalists share similar goals—to uncover truths, to answer questions that need to be asked, and to expose wrongs in the world.

The reporters who covered the "Wet Prince of Bel Air" series, for example, started their project with a simple question—one that had never been asked before. They wanted to understand how it was possible that some people in their region had lush, green properties in a time of severe water shortages. In answering that question, they discovered that certain people were wasting a precious natural resource.

People who read about this water abuse—including politicians—became outraged enough that they demanded change. Because of the "Wet Prince" stories, California now has new laws related to water use and abuse.

Sometimes, the changes that result from investigative journalism projects aren't so swift or obvious. Through their e-waste documentary, Peter Klein and his students raised public awareness about the environmental hazards and human suffering caused by discarded electronics. Since then, many other journalists have reported on related stories, and many countries have created new laws about the disposal of e-waste.

Though they are not people who actively push for it, the work of investigative journalists often leads to change.

Certainly some change has happened. But toxic e-waste dumps continue to exist around the world.

Investigative journalism projects might sometimes lead to global change and awareness, but they often have more of a personal and local impact on people. That was the result of the stories about DuPont and C8. Through Mariah Blake's and Sharon Lerner's articles, members of the public learned about the poisonous impacts of C8 and what they needed to do to protect themselves. People who'd been afraid to speak up were finally heard and, together, demanded change.

DuPont was ordered to clean up the local environment and fund a community health and education program.

Without investigative journalism, the voices of these citizens may never have been heard. Without investigative journalism, politicians and businesspeople might get away with abusing their power. Without investigative journalism, certain crimes might go unsolved, certain wrongs might go uncorrected, and certain secrets might remain hidden.

Investigative journalists tell stories that otherwise might not get told, and those stories often lead to necessary change that might not happen otherwise.

BIBLIOGRAPHY

CHAPTER 1

Chung, Emily. "B.C. students buy sensitive U.S. defence data for $40 in Africa," *CBC News*, December 16, 2009. https://bit.ly/2PLlAHE

"Investigative Journalism." UNESCO, https://bit.ly/2Pc6ERP

Klein, Peter. "Ghana: Digital Dumping Ground." June 23, *FRONTLINE/World*, 2009. www.pbs.org/frontlineworld/stories/ghana804/video/video_index.html

CHAPTER 2

Klein, Peter. "Ghana: Digital Dumping Ground." *FRONTLINE/World*, June 23, 2009. www.pbs.org/frontlineworld/stories/ghana804/video/video_index.html

Klein, Peter. Personal correspondence with author, 2018.

Pinchin, Karen. "UBC j-schoolers expose digital dumping ground." *Maclean's*, June 23, 2009. https://bit.ly/2wroSHX

CHAPTER 3

Baluja, Tamara. "10 tips for the savvy environmental journalist," *J-Source*, 2013. http://j-source.ca/article/10-tips-for-the-savvy-environmental-journalist

Corey, Michael, and Lance Williams. "Who is the Wet Prince of Bel Air? Here are the likely culprits," *Reveal*, September 20, 2016. https://bit.ly/2CaGFbZ

Corey, Michael. "Now this is a story all about how we found the Wet Princes of Bel Air," *Reveal*, September 19, 2016. https://bit.ly/2NxsU87

Society of Environmental Journalists. "Winners: SEJ 16th Annual Awards for Reporting on the Environment," Society of Environmental Journalists, 2017. www.sej.org/winners-sej-16th-annual-awards-reporting-environment#CarmodyLarge

Stevens, Matt. "California's heavy water users could face penalties if drought persists," Los Angeles Times, September 2, 2016. www.latimes.com/local/lanow/la-me-ln-water-wasters-20160831-snap-story.html

Williams, Lance, and Katharine Mieszkowski. "The Wet Prince of Bel Air: Who is California's biggest water guzzler?" Reveal, 2015. https://bit.ly/2LBlgbl

CHAPTER 4

Aton, Adam. "Behind the Story: How a reporter peered inside one of the world's most powerful chemical companies," Investigative Reporters and Editors, October 5, 2015. https://bit.ly/2BZQ45O

Lopate, Leonard. "How DuPont Poisoned West Virginia," *The Leonard Lopate Show*, WNYC radio, September 3, 2015. www.wnyc.org/story/how-dupont-poisoned-west-virginia

Rich, Nathaniel. "The Lawyer Who Became DuPont's Worst Nightmare," *The New York Times Magazine*, January 6, 2016. https://nyti.ms/1Z62adh

LEARNING MORE

BOOKS

Kallen, Stuart A. *Running Dry: The Global Water Crisis*. Twenty-First Century Books, 2015.

Rowell, Rebecca. *Rachel Carson Sparks the Environmental Movement*. Core Library, 2016.

Macfarlane, Colin. *Hit the Headlines: Exciting Journalism Activities for Improving Writing and Thinking Skills*. Routledge, 2012.

WEBSITES

This web page on the Kiddle Encyclopedia website is entitled "Electronic waste facts." It provides information about e-waste, and links to related information. **https://kids.kiddle.co/Electronic_waste**

"So you want to be an investigative journalist" is an 11-minute video in which the British investigative journalist John Sweeney talks about his work. **www.journalism.co.uk/news/ watch-so-you-want-to-be-an-investigative-reporter-/s2/a603814**

Young Reporters for the Environment (YRE) is an environmental organization for youth who want to report, photograph, or record stories about the environment. Near the bottom of this web page are links to three excellent handbooks to help you get started in environmental journalism. **https://environmentaldefence.ca/ yre-student**

LINKS TO ARTICLES IN THIS BOOK

Chapter 1–2

Klein, Peter. "Ghana: Digital Dumping Ground." *FRONTLINE/ World*, 2009. **www.pbs.org/frontlineworld/stories/ ghana804/video/video_index.html**

Chapter 3

Corey, Michael. "Now this is a story all about how we found the Wet Princes of Bel Air," *Reveal*, 2016. **https://bit.ly/2NxsU87**

Corey, Michael, and Lance Williams. "Who is the Wet Prince of Bel Air? Here are the likely culprits," *Reveal*, 2016. **https://bit.ly/2CaGFbZ**

Williams, Lance, and Katharine Mieszkowski. "The Wet Prince of Bel Air: Who is California's biggest water guzzler?" *Reveal*, 2015. **https://bit.ly/2LBlgbl**

Williams, Lance. "California cracks down on its Wet Princes," *Reveal*, 2016. **https://bit.ly/2okQFp2**

Williams, Lance. "LA's mega water users still pumped millions of gallons despite drought," *Reveal*, 2017. **https://bit.ly/2olo0jE**

Chapter 4

Blake, Mariah. "Welcome to Beautiful Parkersburg, West Virginia," *Huffington Post Highline*, 2015. **https://highline. huffingtonpost.com/articles/en/ welcome-to-beautiful-parkersburg**

Lerner, Sharon. "The Teflon Toxin," The *Intercept*, 2015-2018. **https:// theintercept.com/series/the-teflon-toxin**

GLOSSARY

activists People who take action to support a cause

aerial Existing, operating, or happening in the air

algorithm A set of mathematical instructions or rules that calculate an answer to a problem; usually done by a computer

angles A news story's themes or focus

blackmail To demand money from a person in return for not exposing detrimental information about them

budget A plan that shows the amount of money earned and how it will be spent

chaotic Confused, disordered, messy, out of control

circuit boards The "brains" of computers or other electronic devices; a sheet of plastic embedded with metals and electric elements that make the connections a device needs to function

climate change The long-term change in Earth's weather patterns—especially the warming of Earth's temperature, which is caused by human activity

concealed Hidden

conspiracy A secret plan by a group of people to do something illegal or otherwise nasty

consumers People who buy goods and services

copyright Legal rules that protect an author's work; prevents others from copying the work without permission; also applies to music, films, photographs, and other artistic works

court A place where legal matters are debated and decided

cross-checking Confirming something using various sources

data Facts, statistics, or other information

data mining The process of sorting through large amounts of information to find trends, patterns, and relationships

developing nations Countries with a low standard of living compared to many other countries in the world; countries where people typically have low incomes, limited food, medicine, and educational opportunities

documentary A long-form, in-depth investigative report, in video format

graduate students Students who are pursuing an advanced university or college degree

grant An amount of money that is given to someone by a government or company, to be used for a particular purpose

graphic designers Professionals who create and put together visuals for a project

habitat The specialized environments where plants and animals live

immersive Providing information that appeals to a variety of senses, not just sight and sound

industry The people, companies, and activities involved in the making of goods and services for sale

integrity Honesty, honor, ethical principles, high moral standards.

lawsuit A legal claim or dispute that is settled in court by a judge

legal Related to law

markets Places where goods and services are bought and sold

natural resource Something found in nature that is useful to humans, such as water, wood, and coal

nervous system The body parts that transmit messages to and from the brain

nonprofit Not for financial gain

organ A part of the body that has a specific function

painstaking Involving a great deal of time and/or effort

precious metal A rare metal that is worth a lot of money, such as gold

privacy laws Rules that control how personal information can be used

proactive Taking action, rather than waiting for something to happen.

public records Documents available to the general public; includes many different kinds of legal, government, and business documents

radiation The emission of energy waves

recorded history Events of the past that were written down

replicate To copy or repeat

restrictive Limited

satellite An object placed in orbit above Earth, usually to collect information

shard A piece of broken glass, pottery, metal, or other such material

slums Districts of overcrowding and poverty within a city

sources People who provide information to a journalist; documents, videos, recordings, or other publications that provide information to a journalist

territory An area that is under the rule of another country

toxic Poisonous

United Nations An international organization made up of 193 countries that works to promote world peace and human rights

verify To prove that something is true or correct

waste pollution Discarded materials that contaminate the environment

INDEX

ABOUT THE AUTHOR

Diane Dakers has been a print and broadcast journalist since 1991. She specializes in culture, science, and business reporting. She has also written 24 nonfiction and three fiction books for youth.